THE CREATION

The Creation

Written by Janeen Brady
Art by Bonnie Oswald

ISBN 13: 978-1-59955-139-5

Published by CFI, an imprint of Cedar Fort, Inc.
2373 W. 700 S., Springville, UT, 84663
Distributed by Cedar Fort, Inc., www.cedarfort.com

Library of Congress Cataloging-in-Publication Data

Brady, Janeen.
  The Creation / written by Janeen Brady ; art by Bonnie Oswald.
    p. cm.
  ISBN 978-1-59955-139-5
  1. Creation–Juvenile poetry. 2. Children's poetry, American. I. Oswald, Bonnie, ill. II. Title.

  PS3602.R3434C74 2008
  811'.6–dc22

                                    2008003604

Jacket design by Nicole Williams
Book design by Bonnie Oswald
Jacket design © 2008 by Lyle Mortimer
Printed on acid-free paper

Printed in Hong Kong
10 9 8 7 6 5 4 3 2 1

Dedicated to our Grandchildren
And all other children who believe in God

THE CREATION

Before there was music or rhythm or rhyme,
    And even before the creation of time,
Before there were oceans or land with its features,
Or anything in them, for there were no creatures,

A Father looked down on the wide, open space
And said, "I know just what to do in this place."
But that was before anything came to be,
Before there was you; even long before me.

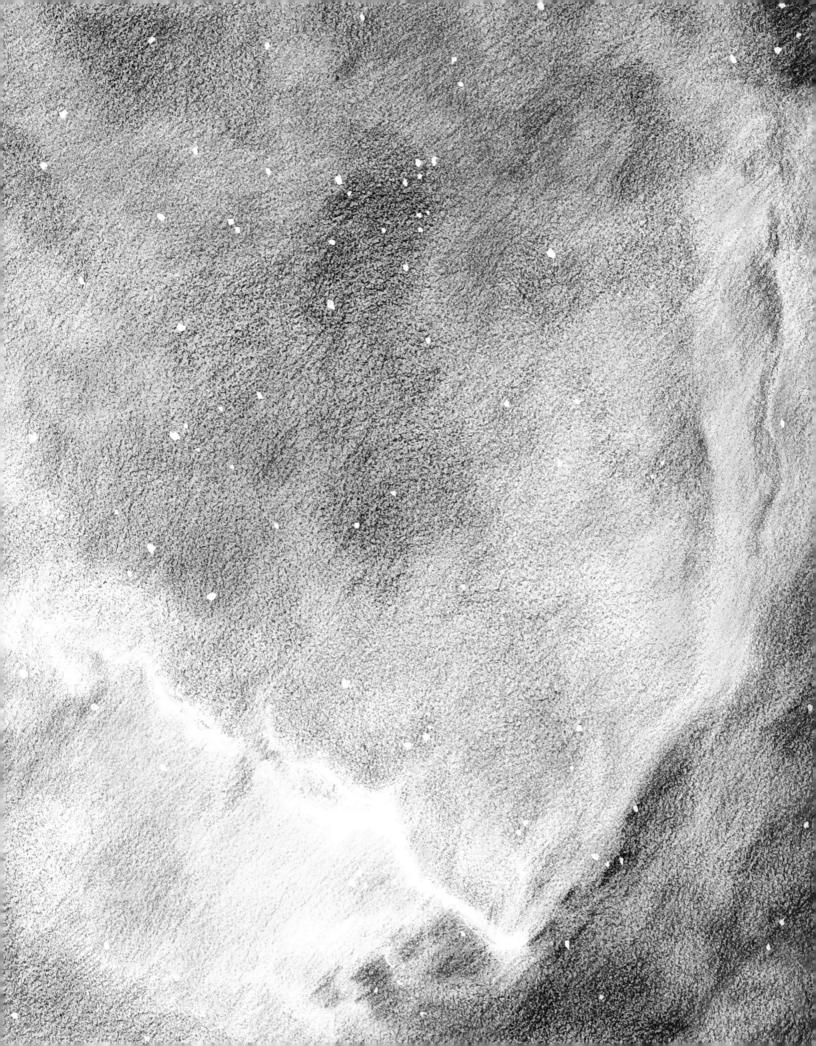

o he started in thinking and planning his plan,
And what he envisioned was wonderfully grand.
He'd need to make heavens that reach up so high
And go on forever to fill up the sky,
For God knew that there was an endless expanse,
And that sort of thing must be planned in advance.

H e thought of a world filled
with sunshine and air
And other things people would need to live there,
"And I'll make it good," He said, "so when they see
My lovely creation, they might think of me."

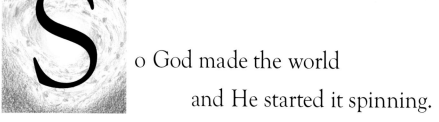 o God made the world
and He started it spinning.
"Oh my," He exclaimed. "This is quite a beginning."
But it was a world that was formless and void,
And certainly no place that could be enjoyed.

All covered with darkness, as dark as could be,
He had to do something or no one could see.
So with His great power and wisdom and might
God stretched forth His hands and said,

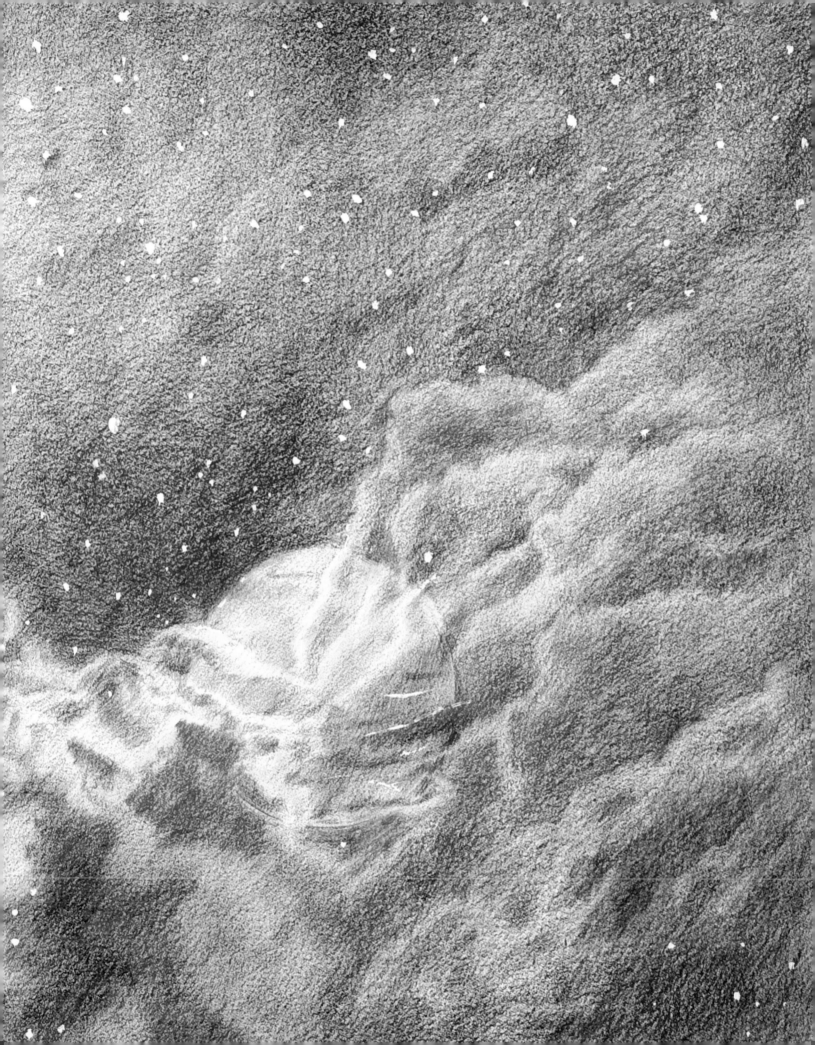

"Let there be light."

And the evening and the morning were the first day.
Genesis 1:5

Then what God did next seems quite strange, we admit it,
But it's in the Bible so we know He did it.
He made a huge blanket, which He put in place
To cover the earth as it hurtles through space.

He called it the firmament; that's an odd word.
We call it the atmosphere; that's one you've heard,
With waters above it, and waters below,
Waters that turn into rain, even snow.

And the evening and the morning were the second day.
Genesis 1 :8

He gathered the waters on earth all together,
And dry land appeared so He could tell whether
The grass and the herb and the fruit trees would grow.
They certainly did, because God made it so.

But how could they not with His thousands of seeds
And how could He help but be very well pleased.
The earth was now green and beginning to yield
In plentiful, glorious field after field.

**And the
evening and the morning were the third day.**
Genesis 1:13

But there was no moon in the sky
and no sun,
No stars in the heavens, no, not even one,
And there was no daytime or nighttime at all,

No summer,   no winter,

no spring,   and no fall.

he earth plainly needed a heavenly light
  And something to separate daytime from night,
For otherwise there'd be no way to tell time.
God needed to make a celestial sign.

So God made the sun, and He made it so bright
It covered the earth with a dazzling light,
And then for the nighttime He fashioned the moon
And also the stars; there was plenty of room.

**H**e set them for signs and for years
and for seasons,
For days and for nights, and for all of these reasons
He felt very satisfied, anyone would,
For so far He knew His creation was good.

And the evening and the morning were the fourth day.
Genesis 1:19

The oceans were heaving,
        the waves crashing in,
When God said, "It's time for new life to begin."
For He had prepared in the depths of the deep
The forces of life that would no longer sleep.

Then as He commanded there soon came to be
The wonderful creatures that live in the sea.
In colors and sizes and shapes of all kinds,
Just to behold them would boggle your mind.

All covered with fins and with gills and with scales,
The tiniest slugs to the mightiest whales.
And God made them all, any kind you could wish,

Hundreds and thousands

and millions of fish.

While seas full of fish were a wonderful sight,
   Skies that were empty just didn't seem right.
Of course there were clouds; clouds are beautiful things,
But God knew the sky needed something with wings,

Something that warbles a joyful sound
And lives in a nest in a tree on the ground,
For He could envision the fowl who would fly
High over the earth like a breeze through the sky.

The wings He would give them
could stretch out and glide
Or flutter or flap or else tuck up inside.
He carefully planned them, the beautiful birds,
Those marvelous creatures too lovely for words.

Pink ones and white ones and blue ones and red,
Black ones and yellow ones, and then instead
Of scales they'd have feathers, all fluffy and soft
And light as the air to help keep them aloft,
To soar and to sing in the beautiful blue.
"Oh yes, I'll make birds," He said. "That's what I'll do."

And then He commanded they all multiply
And replenish the earth, filling waters and sky.

And the evening and the morning were the fifth day.
Genesis 1:23

I t was astounding the things God had done,
But even more so knowing what was to come,
For there were whole continents, acres of land,
And so far no creatures with four legs to stand
Or slide on their bellies or hang by their tails
Or crawl, oh so softly, like even, well, snails.

But now He would fill all the jungles and swamps,
The highlands and lowlands with life that could romp
Or gallop or slither or wiggle or hop
Or burrow or climb, even some that could stalk.
It all would take time, a long time I admit,
But, since He was God, He had plenty of it.

So first He designed them
                and then He made cattle
With hooves and with horns that could make you skedaddle
If you got too close while they foraged for food,
For a bull that's upset can be terribly rude.

Then like it or not He made things that would squirm,
Like creepies and crawlies; He even made worms.
There must be a reason why bugs had to be,
But bugs I like best are the ones far from me.

He made so many beasts, almost a million,
From smallest to largest, perhaps a gazillion,
Some most ferocious and dangerously wild,
And some that would make a fine pet for a child.
The fish and the beasts and the creeping things too
Were more than enough to fill up a zoo.

Next He commanded the cattle and beasts
To bring forth their kind so that they could increase
And bless all the earth with both raiment and food.
And God saw it all, and He said it was good.

ow it was all finished—well, practically so—
There was just one more creation to go,
One more amazing work, God's very best,
The absolute ultimate; then He could rest.

He'd form a new species, designed to be free
To reason and think and be all they could be,
Not governed by instincts without any choice.
This one would be higher; this one would have voice,
To choose right or wrong, but hopefully right,
For goodness, you know, is God's greatest delight.

So God fashioned man in His very own image,
And you, my dear child, claim this royal lineage
Because we all came from this very first man,
God's noblest work since creation began.

God called the man Adam; that's how he
was known,
And God said, "It's not good the man is alone.
I'll fashion a woman, the beautiful Eve,
The loveliest creature a God can perceive."

And when Adam saw her, surrounded by light,
His heart skipped a beat. It was love at first sight.

And then God united them, husband and wife,
The first of all families in this mortal life.

And the evening and the morning were the sixth day.

Genesis 1:31

In the Garden of Eden,
        a land filled with flowers,
They made their first home, where they spent happy hours
In innocent pleasures, for there was no sin
In this place God had chosen for us to begin.

Butthen came temptation,
and then came the Fall.
And they had to leave Eden and that changed it all.
But we'll save that story for some other time.
Perhaps we will find it in some other rhyme.

So what is the moral?   It simply is this:
We didn't just happen to somehow exist.
The earth and the sky and all that we see
Didn't happen by chance, but through Deity.

For all of creation was under His care,
From the very beginning, our Father was there
Perfecting each step with divine overseeing
As all of the universe came into being.

So worship and serve Him, our God high above us,
And know all He did was for us, for He loves us.

THE BEGINNING